TRAIN YOUR BRAIN

THINK

LIKE AN

ARTIST

Written by Alex Woolf

illustrated by David Broadbent

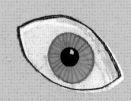

CRABTREE
PUBLISHING COMPANY
WWW.CRABTREEBOOKS.COM

CRABTREE
PUBLISHING COMPANY
WWW.CRABTREEBOOKS.COM

A note from the author and publisher
In preparation of this book, all due care has been exercised with regard to the instructions, activities, and techniques depicted. The publishers and author regret that they can accept no liability for any loss or injury sustained. Always get adult supervision and follow manufacturers' advice when using electric and battery-powered appliances.

The activities described in this book should always be done in the presence of a trusted adult. A trusted adult is a person (over 18 years old) in a child's life who makes them feel safe, comfortable, and supported. It might be a parent, teacher, family friend, care worker, or another adult.

Every effort has been made by the publishers to ensure websites are suitable for children, that they are of the highest educational value, and that they contain no inappropriate or offensive material. However, because of the nature of the Internet, it is impossible to guarantee that the contents of these sites will not be altered. We strongly advise that Internet access is supervised by a responsible adult.

Facts, figures, and dates were correct when going to press.

First published in Great Britain in 2021 by Wayland

Copyright © Hodder and Stoughton, 2021

Author: Alex Woolf
Illustrator: David Broadbent
Series editor: Melanie Palmer
Series design: David Broadbent
Editorial director: Kathy Middleton
Editor: Kathy Middleton
Proofreader: Crystal Sikkens
Production technician: Margaret Salter
Print coordinator: Katherine Berti

Library and Archives Canada Cataloguing in Publication

CIP available at Library and Archives Canada

Library of Congress Cataloging-in-Publication Data

CIP available at the Library of Congress

Crabtree Publishing Company

www.crabtreebooks.com   1-800-387-7650

Published by Crabtree Publishing Company in 2022.

Printed in the U.S.A./012022/CG20210915

Published in Canada
Crabtree Publishing
616 Welland Ave.
St. Catharines, Ontario
L2M 5V6

Published in the United States
Crabtree Publishing
347 Fifth Ave
Suite 1402-145
New York, NY 10016

CONTENTS

What Is Art?

Art is anything we create that is pleasing or interesting to look at.
It could be a painting, drawing, **collage**, or **sculpture**.

Art can be an image we have made of something we've seen.

It can also express what we feel, imagine, and dream.

We make art for many different reasons.

Here are some of them:
- to make our surroundings more beautiful
- to record and celebrate events and individuals
- to inspire and encourage others
- to communicate ideas
- to express our religious beliefs.

We make art all the time, sometimes without even realizing it. Whenever we doodle something on a notepad, snap a photo of something we like, or build a sandcastle or a snowman, we are creating art.

The urge to produce art is a natural one and part of what makes us human. Humans have been making art for many thousands of years.

Art teaches us many important things, such as how to observe, plan, and solve problems. It teaches us about colors, shapes, and **textures**. It also teaches us about patience and resilience and not giving up.

Art is about so much more than creating something attractive to hang on your wall. The final product may look good, but the really fun part is the journey.

In this book, we'll look at ways of developing your creative mind so you can start to think like an artist.

Use Your Eyes

The first thing an artist must learn to do is observe, because the world out there is where we get our inspiration and ideas. To think like an artist, always pay attention to what is around you and keep your mind open.

Normally, when we look at something, we just think...

That's a banana.

That's a bone... Yum!

As artists we must try looking at things more closely. Choose an object and imagine it is the first time you've ever seen anything like it. Break it down into a list of features.

Here's an example of the features of an apple.

Find some other objects and try describing their features in a similar way.

apple	
color	red
shape	round
texture	smooth
hardness	firm
shininess	gleaming

Remember, the way you see the world is unique to you. Everyone interprets the world in their own way.

When you look at an object, ask yourself what it reminds you of. You'll see things in a leaf or a cloud or an ink blot that others won't.

Go out into your neighborhood and look for things that might inspire you. It could be a twig, pebble, pinecone, leaf, feather, or acorn.

Take a bag with you to collect some of the things you find.

There may be some things that you can't take back home with you, such as an animal or an interesting-looking tree. Take photos of the things you can't collect. You could even use paper and pencil or chalk to make a bark rubbing.

The important thing is to open your eyes to all the fascinating and beautiful objects in the world around you.

Find the Beauty

We aren't all lucky enough to have a spectacular view outside our window for us to paint. As artists we need to learn to appreciate the beauty of everyday objects and scenes.

Beauty can be found in some unexpected places. For example:

- a rusty car
- a cobweb
- a weed sprouting from cracked pavement
- a muddy puddle
- a rotting apple

Often what's most interesting isn't the object itself, but what you see in it.

For example, take a staircase. Look at the lines and angles in the steps and the banister rails. Look at the shadows they form.

Anything that is interesting in your eyes can be a subject for art, no matter how ordinary.

It all comes down to your mindset. If you decide that everything in your house is boring because you've seen it all before, then it WILL be boring.

But if you try to keep an open mind, you might start seeing everyday objects with fresh eyes.

Imagine you're an alien who has just arrived on this planet. It's the first time you've seen any of these objects. How would they appear to you?

You might notice that a jug has a beautiful curved shape. A corkscrew has an interesting spiral pattern. A chess piece has a pleasing shape made up of curves and straight edges.

Try looking at the objects around you with "new eyes." You'll find a surprising number of beautiful things to draw or paint.

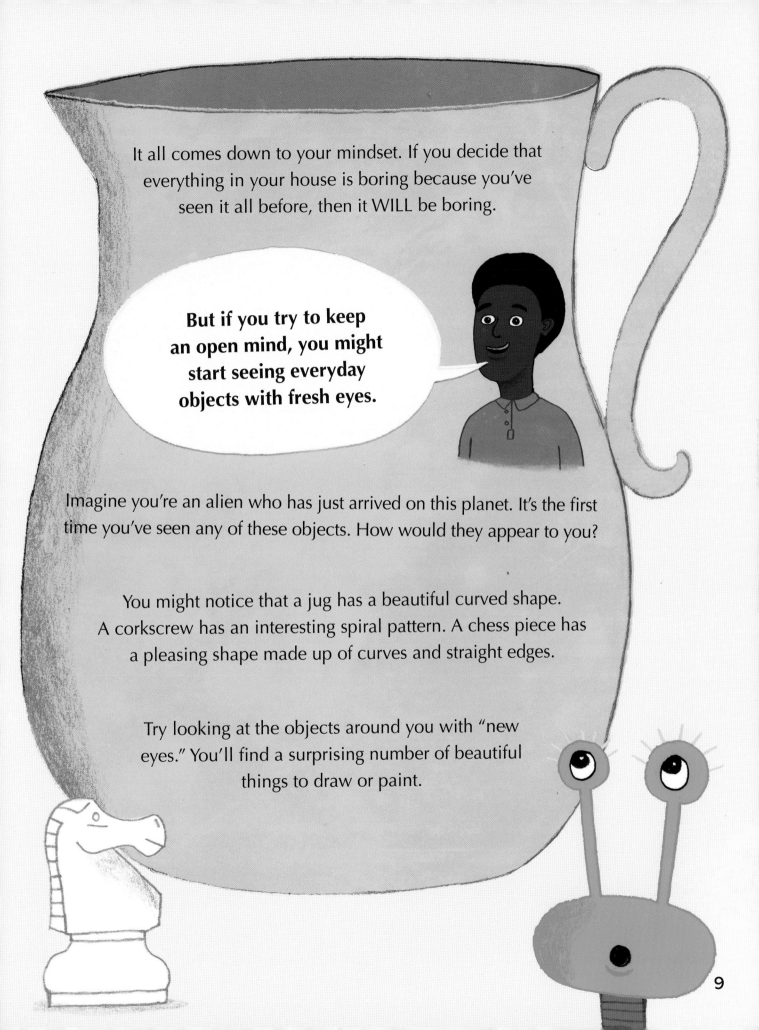

Rembrandt van Rijn: Dutch Artist

Rembrandt was born on July 15, 1606, in Leiden, the Netherlands. His father was a miller, his mother was a baker's daughter, and he was their ninth child. After receiving a good education, he left school at around 14 to train as an artist. Rembrandt became an apprentice to the artist Jacob van Swaneburgh and also received lessons from another artist, Pieter Lastman.

Rembrandt quickly became known as a skillful painter. He opened his own art studio in 1625, when he was just 19. In 1631, Rembrandt moved to the city of Amsterdam where he began earning a living by painting portraits of wealthy people. In the days before cameras, portrait painters were much in demand. He became known as a great portrait artist. He also painted over 40 portraits of himself and his family.

Rembrandt was one of the first portrait painters to capture people's personalities and emotions. He didn't just show his subjects in a flattering light as many portrait artists did. He painted them as they actually looked, which was a **radical** approach for the time. He was especially skilled at using light and shadow to illustrate mood.

In spite of his success, Rembrandt's personal life was filled with tragedy. In 1634, he married Saskia van Uylenburg. Their first three children died shortly after they were born. Only their fourth child, Titus, born in 1641, survived to adulthood. Saskia died in 1642, probably from **tuberculosis**. Rembrandt's drawings of her when she was sick are among his most moving works.

Rembrandt also painted landscapes and scenes from the Bible. One of his most famous works is *The Night Watch*. The painting is very big—12 x 14 feet (3.6 x 4.4 m). It is remarkable for its use of light and shade and its **composition**. Instead of having the 18 soldiers lined up, Rembrandt chose to have each one doing something different, turning it into an action painting.

Rembrandt died on October 4, 1669. Over the course of his life, he produced almost 300 paintings, as well as many drawings and etchings. He was a huge influence on other artists and is regarded today as one of the greatest artists in history.

Connect and Combine

Artists often connect and combine different things to create an interesting or dramatic effect. One way they do this is through collage: layering and then gluing different materials on a flat surface.

A collage can be a picture of something or just a pattern.

The most interesting collages combine a variety of materials, colors, patterns, and textures to create an overall effect. If you think about it, nature does this all the time. A tree might be made up of hard, rough, bumpy, brown bark, and soft, smooth, shiny green leaves.

When the combination is unusual, this is called juxtaposition. This can be done by pairing contrasting shapes textures, or colors.

Juxtaposition can also be done by contrasting the subject with the material you make it from. For instance, if you make a butterfly out of steel nuts and bolts, this might surprise viewers because butterflies are soft and delicate and nuts and bolts are just the opposite. The Swiss artist Méret Oppenheim used juxtaposition when she created a teacup made of fur.

Try creating a collage out of
pieces of paper and fabric.

Take your time when choosing materials to use.
Look for contrasts such as warm and cool colors,
straight and curved edges, rough and smooth
textures, or dull and shiny surfaces. Natural objects,
such as dried leaves, pine needles, and twigs and
seeds, can make a great addition to any collage.

Try arranging different combinations
on the paper before you glue anything.

You could create a simple
pattern, or try to recreate a
favorite place, special event, or
a memory. You could even try
spelling out your name.

Reuse Old Materials

As an artist, it helps to be creative with the materials you use. The most unusual objects can become materials for your art. Things that might otherwise end up in the garbage can still be used with a bit of imagination.

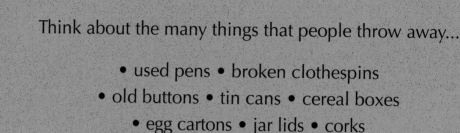

Think about the many things that people throw away...

- used pens • broken clothespins
- old buttons • tin cans • cereal boxes
- egg cartons • jar lids • corks
- cartons • magazines
- plastic bottles

Thinking like an artist means looking at such objects in a new way and not as things with only one function. Instead, it means viewing them as objects with particular features that could find a new life in a work of art.

Artwork created by reusing old objects is called upcycled art. Viewers will be impressed not only with the art itself, but with the imagination you used in putting it together from these old materials. On top of that, you're helping to save the planet!

Remember: always make sure the materials you reuse are clean and don't have sharp edges.

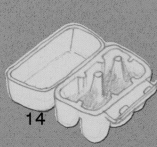

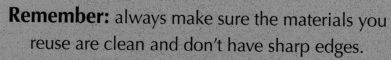

Tin can windchimes

Here's an upcycled art project you can try yourself.

You will need:
- 3 or 5 clean tin cans
- acrylic paints and paintbrushes
- string
- hammer and nail
- metal washers or nuts
- tape

1. Soak the cans in warm water to remove any labels.

2. Put tape around the rims of the cans to cover up any sharp edges. Ask an adult to help with this part.

3. Paint the outside of the tin cans in different colors.

4. Ask an adult to use the hammer and nail to punch a hole in the bottom of each can.

5. Thread a length of string through each hole, and tie two washers or nuts to the end inside the can. One of the washers or nuts should be tied higher up to hold the string in place. The other should be tied near the end so it dangles and can make a noise knocking against the inside of the can.

6. Hang up the cans together in a breezy outdoor place. Make sure they're all touching.

When the wind blows, your tin can windchimes will make a clanking sound as they knock together.

Learn from Great Artists

We all want to be original, but as artists we should always be willing to learn from and be inspired by great artists of the past. Not only can they teach us lessons with their techniques, but also with their approaches to life.

Wow!

Harriet Powers (1837–1910) was a skilled quilt maker. Born into slavery near Athens, Georgia, and later **emancipated**, Powers turned African American folktales, historical events, and Bible stories into powerful pictures. She then sewed them onto quilts. This approach was unusual for the time. Powers showed how a self-educated Black woman could create a unique form of art.

Paul Cézanne (1839–1906) was a great French artist who worked for years without much recognition. He only found success late in life. He teaches us the importance of perseverance.

Austrian artist **Tina Blau** (1845–1916) was a talented landscape painter who attempted new approaches to painting light and air. Due to attitudes at the time, many refused to take her seriously and believed a man was helping her. Blau's life demonstrates how artists must often struggle against the **prejudices** of others.

French artist **Suzanne Valadon** (1865–1938) showed how sometimes it helps to ignore the rules of art. She was an artist's model who became a famous artist herself, especially painting female figures. She lacked formal training and didn't follow normal approaches. Her powerful, emotional works were sneered at by many male art critics. Yet she had four major exhibitions in her career.

Pablo Picasso (1881–1973) found success early and could easily have continued creating the same kind of art all his life. Instead, every few years, he would try out a new style. In all, he went through seven key phases as an artist. This teaches us that we should never stop experimenting with our art.

Next time you go to an art gallery, find an artist you admire. Try to create artwork in the same style.

Frida Kahlo: Mexican Artist

Frida Kahlo, one of North America's greatest painters, was born on July 6, 1907, in Coyocoan, Mexico City, Mexico. When she was six, she caught a disease called polio. It damaged her right leg and caused her to walk with a limp. Despite this, she had an active childhood, playing soccer, swimming, and wrestling. She also enjoyed painting.

In 1922, Kahlo enrolled at the well-regarded National Preparatory School in Mexico City. She wanted to become a doctor. One day, when she was 18, she was in a terrible accident when a bus she was riding in collided with a streetcar. Kahlo was badly injured with fractures to her spine and pelvis. She would suffer bouts of severe pain for the rest of her life.

While Kahlo was recovering, she returned to her childhood hobby of painting. Her mother had a special easel made for her so she could paint in bed. Kahlo discovered she had a passion for art and decided to devote her life to it. During her career, she painted many portraits of herself. Of her 143 paintings, 55 of them were self-portraits. She used these to express her emotional state, such as her feelings about not being able to have children.

Like all great artists, Kahlo found inspiration in the world around her, including the culture and politics of Mexico and in the work of other artists. Strongly influenced by traditional Mexican art, Kahlo's paintings were bright and colorful and filled with patterns and symbols. She would often depict herself in traditional Mexican clothing and hairstyles. She would also include monkeys, parrots, dogs, and deer in her self-portraits.

In 1929, Kahlo married another famous Mexican painter, Diego Rivera. Their relationship was not a smooth one and they separated several times. But they always went back to each other. Meanwhile, Kahlo's fame grew, and in the 1930s, she began to exhibit in places such as New York and Paris. Her art was a mixture of realism, which depicted the world truthfully, and symbolism, which focused on illustrating ideas.

By 1950, her health had deteriorated. She had to have a number of operations and was confined to her bed for long periods. Yet she continued to paint. Frida Kahlo died of a blood clot on July 13, 1954. She was just 47 years old. Her reputation grew after her death. Many were inspired by her art as well as her moving life story.

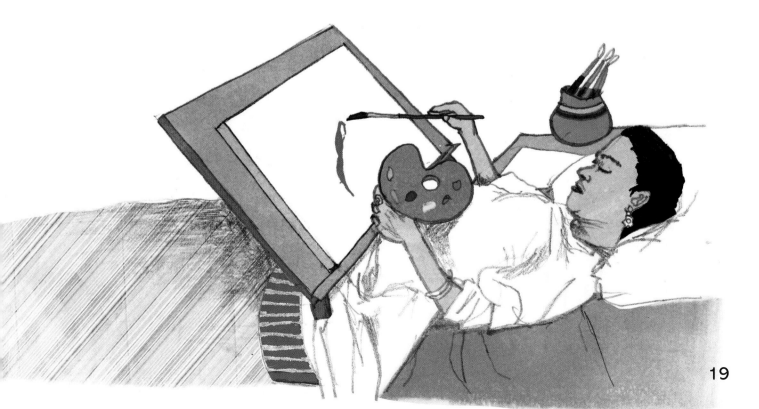

Plan Carefully

Once you have found a subject for your art, you need to start thinking
in a more practical way about how you are going to create it.

First, you should plan the composition. If you are painting or drawing a still life,
which is a grouping of objects, look for a variety of shapes, colors, and textures.
Think about how to place the different objects so they attract the viewer's eye.

Think about the negative space, which is the space around and between
the objects. If you fill in your picture everywhere and leave too little negative
space, the picture might be too overwhelming to the viewer. On the other hand,
leaving too much negative space could make your artwork look dull.

Consider where you place the focal
point of your artwork. The focal point
is the most interesting and eye-catching
part. Your composition is likely to be
more interesting if the focal point isn't
exactly in the center of the artwork.
Placing it one-third of the way from the
sides, top, or bottom adds more interest.

Another rule to remember is that odd numbers can be more interesting than even numbers. If you are drawing a group of people, it is better to draw three or five people, not four or six.

Decide on the right tools and materials for your artwork. For a drawing, it is good to have a range of hard and soft pencils. For a painting, you might need two or three sizes of brush, so you can paint in both broad and fine strokes. Check to make sure you have all the paint colors you will need.

Once you are ready, don't just launch into your artwork. Practicing will help you get better. Use scrap paper to try out different colors. If it's a collage, try placing pieces together to see how they look before attaching them with glue.

The more carefully you plan, the better your artwork should turn out.

Practice Regularly

To be an accomplished artist, you need to practice. This means doing similar actions again and again until you become better at them. Regular practice will make your hand movements more precise and give you better coordination between your hands and your eyes.

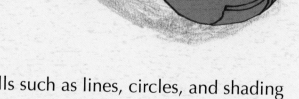

I try to practice every day.

Keep a small sketchpad with you at all times so you can practice drawing wherever you are. If you're sitting on the bus, try sketching what you see out the window. If you're watching TV, pause the screen at an interesting scene and sketch that.

When practicing, try starting with core skills such as lines, circles, and shading before moving on to the things you struggle with.

If you find faces hard, break it down and practice noses, mouths, ears, and eyes in separate sessions. To liven up your practice, choose a different theme or object each day.

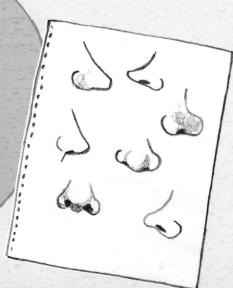

A fun way of practicing art is through doodling.

Try randomly sketching anything that comes to mind. This is good for coordination and helps you to process thoughts and ideas in your head. You can often surprise yourself with the images you come up with. They may even give you ideas for a new piece of art.

If you need a way of kickstarting your imagination, try filling a piece of paper with randomly placed dots. Then connect the dots with curved or straight lines to create a pattern or object.

Experiment

You may be tempted to stick to what you know in art. Perhaps if you try something new, you will fail at it and people will doubt your talent. This is called fixed-mindset thinking. As an artist you should be bold about trying new things and going beyond your comfort zone.

Art is all about trial and error—finding out what works and what doesn't. You need to experiment to progress.

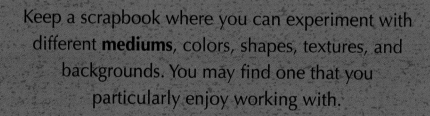

Keep a scrapbook where you can experiment with different **mediums**, colors, shapes, textures, and backgrounds. You may find one that you particularly enjoy working with.

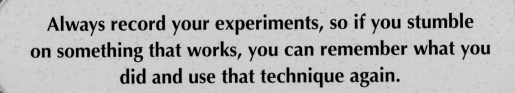

Always record your experiments, so if you stumble on something that works, you can remember what you did and use that technique again.

Experiment by creating a drawing in charcoal. It can be messy and more difficult to work with than pencil, but it does produce beautiful, rich effects. Charcoal is particularly good for **contrasting** light and dark. Here are some tips:

- Don't press too hard: use a lighter touch than with a pencil, except for the darkest parts of your drawing.

- Smudge it with your finger or a cotton swab to create tones that gradually change.

- Use an eraser and combine it with chalk to create **highlights**.

- Use hairspray to set the charcoal so it doesn't smear. Ask an adult to help with this part.

Make Mistakes

Not all your attempts at art will be a success—and that's fine. It doesn't mean you're a bad artist. Your failures are just as important as your successes, if you are prepared to learn from them.

You may not want to display them on your wall for everyone to see, but they are all part of the process of becoming a good artist.

Just because you don't like something you've painted or drawn, that doesn't make you bad at art. Take note of what you did, try to figure out what went wrong, and use that new knowledge as a springboard for when you tackle your next work.

Don't set unrealistic expectations or think you can produce something amazing on your first attempt. This will always lead to frustration and disappointment. Instead, set realistic targets.

Don't compare yourself to the great artists or even the most talented artist in your class. Even the best artist was once a child producing scribbles. Instead of comparing yourself to them, focus on your own work.

Keep your previous work and date it so you can see your own development. You may be surprised at how much you improve over time.

I'm much better than I used to be!

Review Your Work

No one knows better than you what you were trying to achieve with your artwork. If you were trying to draw a cat and everyone thinks it's a dog, only you will know the truth! This makes you the ideal person to **review** your art.

Review your work as you progress with it. Every few minutes take a step back and try to look at it with fresh eyes. Check it against the object you are drawing. Are the **proportions** right? What about the light and shade, or the colors if it's a painting?

Review your work again once you complete it. The first rule to remember: no negative criticism. Check the following:

1. What did you do well?

2. What could you improve?

3. Compared to your previous work, what went better and what went worse? Is there anything consistently lacking in all your work?

Try writing a checklist to use with all your future artwork. When writing it, think about all the things you feel you'd like to improve about your art. If there's something you struggle with, put it on the list.

Sample Checklist	
• Am I choosing the right colors for the work or just the colors I like the best?	**6**
• Am I getting the proportions right?	**8**
• Am I getting the **perspective** right?	**7**
• Am I achieving a good **tonal** range of light and shade?	**5**
• Am I drawing what I see or what I think should be there?	**7**

Use your checklist with every artwork you create. Give yourself a score out of ten for each item and see how you improve over time.

Wu Guanzhong: Chinese Artist

Wu Guanzhong was born in 1919, in Jiangsu province, in eastern China. In 1936, he enrolled at the National Academy of Art in Hangzhou. There, he was taught Chinese and **Western** painting by several top Chinese artists, including Lin Fengmian, who stirred an ambition in him to study in Paris, France.

Wu eventually traveled to Paris in 1947. He spent three years there studying at a prestigious art school. He was particularly drawn to the works of the painters Cézanne, Gauguin, and Van Gogh.

Wu returned to China in 1950, where he began teaching aspects of Western art to students in Beijing. The fashion in Chinese art at this time, encouraged by the new communist government, was called socialist realism. Some criticized Wu for introducing Western art ideas, but he did not listen.

In 1966, a political upheaval began in China called the Cultural Revolution. Foreign ideas and traditional Western and Chinese art styles were outlawed. In fear, Wu destroyed many of his Western works. The government banned him from painting for years. In 1973, as the Cultural Revolution eased, Wu began to paint again. Over the next decades he became one of China's most celebrated artists. He died in Beijing on June 25, 2010.

Wu described himself as "a snake swallowing an elephant." The snake represented the Chinese artist in him, and the elephant symbolized Western influence. He learned about color and composition from Western painters and combined this with the lightness of touch and tonal variations of Chinese **ink-wash** painting. Wu believed his task as an artist was to recognize the beauty in images and to express this beauty in his paintings.

He painted plants, animals, and people, but is best known for his landscapes and waterscapes. His early work was naturalistic, which means imitating real life. His style became more **abstract** as he got older. He has been described as "an artist of feeling rather than fact."

Wu Guanzhong's life serves as an example to artists everywhere not simply to follow current fashions, but to pursue their vision no matter what others say.

Ask for Help

Everyone gets stuck sometimes. You may think asking for help is a sign of failure or stupidity, or that others might laugh at you. You might feel that you are burdening someone with your questions.

I need help!

The truth is, people who care about you will want to help you. **You just need to ask.**

Believing you're not good enough or worrying about what others may think is fixed mindset thinking. Having a growth mindset means knowing that, through effort and with the help of others, you can overcome your problems and be a better artist.

To achieve success, you need to ask questions and invite feedback. So don't avoid criticism, seek it out. Get teachers and fellow students to look at your work and give you their honest opinions.

Asking for help can start a conversation, which can help you feel like you aren't tackling a problem alone. You may find that others are struggling with the same issues, too.

Sometimes you might not know exactly what's wrong with a piece of artwork, only that it's not quite right. Don't let that stop you from asking for help. A more experienced artist might be able to spot what the problem is.

Some students learn faster than others. That's inevitable. Instead of feeling envious of them, why not try making use of their knowledge by asking them questions and finding out how they do it.

You never know, one day, people might be coming to you for help!

Work with Others

You may picture a typical artist as someone working alone, but artists also work together to create bigger or **mixed-media** artwork.

Maybe the project you have in mind, such as a big **mural**, is too big for one person. Or maybe it requires more than one skill, such as a mobile of painted **origami** birds, a painted sculpture, or a collage of paintings and photos.

Working with others is fun, but very different from working alone. You have to be prepared to:

- listen
- communicate
- manage differences of opinion
- sacrifice some of what you want in order to satisfy the group's aims.

Remember to give praise and encouragement to other team members for their work. Talk positively about the project, and help raise team spirit.

A team art project needs careful planning. To make sure it goes smoothly, follow these stages:

1. Agree on your ultimate goal: what will the finished artwork look like?

2. Agree on your working process: will there be a leader or will you make decisions as a group?

3. Make sure each person knows—and is happy with—their role in the process.

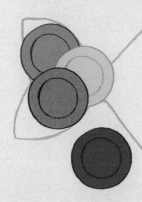

Team up with some friends or classmates and try brainstorming an idea as a group. It could be anything, as long as it's fairly big and can be broken up into different tasks. For example, you could decide to create a **mosaic** of bottle caps or a fish with scales of painted paper plates.

Brainstorming rules:

• no negative comments

• build on others' ideas

• encourage wild ideas

• stay focused

• only one conversation at a time.

Give and Receive Feedback

However far you develop as an artist, you can always learn from others. And as you grow in experience, you can start to offer advice and feedback yourself. Friends and fellow students will see things in your work that you can't see, and vice versa.

That looks great because...

We've all faced similar challenges when we do art, and some people may have found practical solutions they can pass on. Sometimes it's great just to give and receive encouragement.

When giving feedback, always begin by pointing out what you think is successful about the artwork. That will start the conversation off on a positive note.

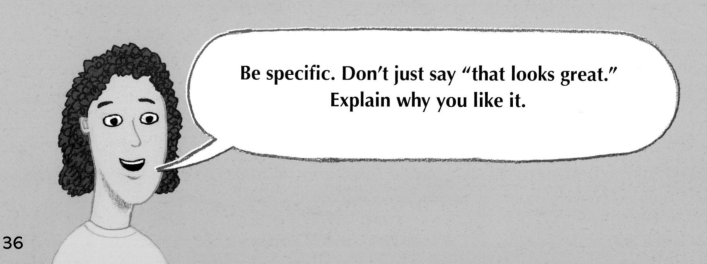

Be specific. Don't just say "that looks great." Explain why you like it.

Avoid negative criticism. Say things like, "Your subject is beautiful. It looks like you are still working on the background. What are you planning to add there?" This will encourage the artist to examine their own work without feeling negative about it.

When receiving feedback, listen carefully to what others are saying, then thank them for it. Sometimes it helps to summarize what they have said back to them. This helps ensure you have understood the feedback correctly.

Ask follow-up questions about anything you're not clear about. Not everything others say will be helpful. Accept what you agree with, but don't feel that you have to agree with everything. It's ultimately your artwork and your decision.

What exactly did you mean by... ?

Try giving and receiving feedback on your latest artwork with a friend.

Georgia O'Keeffe: American Artist

Georgia O'Keeffe is one of the most important artists of the 20th century. She was born in Wisconsin, in 1887, and grew up on a farm. From age 12, she knew she wanted to be an artist. After graduating from high school in 1905, O'Keeffe enrolled at the Art Institute of Chicago. There she studied the traditional techniques of painting.

In 1912, O'Keeffe was inspired by the radical ideas of artist and designer Arthur Wesley Dow. He emphasized the importance of composition, or how you arrange shapes and colors. An important stage in any artist's development is experimenting to find one's own style. O'Keeffe began experimenting with **abstract art**. This is art that expresses feelings through shapes, colors, and marks. O'Keeffe developed a unique style that was a combination of abstract and realistic. A painting of hills, for example, would be used to convey her feelings and ideas.

Her drawings came to the attention of an art dealer, Alfred Stieglitz, who organized an exhibition of O'Keeffe's work in 1916. During the 1920s, O'Keeffe's fame grew.

In 1929, O'Keeffe began visiting northern parts of New Mexico. She fell in love with its deserts and rugged mountains and she eventually made her home there. Her car became her mobile studio as she traveled around, drawing and painting the landscapes and camping out under the stars. O'Keeffe was particularly fascinated by the bones and skulls she found in the desert. "To me they are as beautiful as anything I know," she said.

In the 1950s, O'Keeffe began to travel the world, painting landscapes in Peru and Japan. In 1960, at the age of 73, she began a series of paintings of aerial views of clouds and the sky. In the last years of her life, O'Keeffe's eyesight failed. Despite this, she continued to paint with the help of assistants. She died on March 6, 1986, at age 98.

Georgia O'Keeffe was a pioneer of abstract art famed for her striking paintings of flowers, desert landscapes, and skulls. At a time when the art world was dominated by men, she was one of the first female artists to win international acclaim from both critics and the general public.

Set Yourself Goals

Life as an artist may seem easy and glamorous. But, to be successful, you need to work hard and know how to focus. You need to be productive and be able to meet deadlines. It is worth developing these habits early.

Think about how productive you are. When you're painting, how much time do you ACTUALLY spend painting?

If you have to rush to meet a deadline, you will probably never produce your best work. It's better to pace yourself. One way to do that is to set yourself realistic daily goals of what you want to achieve.

Interruptions can ruin your flow, causing you to make mistakes and be less productive. So turn off your phone and the TV and try to work in a quiet place with no distractions.

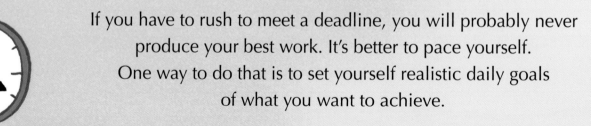

In setting yourself a deadline to finish an artwork, remember to build in break times. You need to take regular refreshment and exercise breaks to keep yourself fresh and focused. If you work for too long at a stretch, the quality of your work is bound to suffer.

Setting goals and deadlines can also help you work more efficiently. Sometimes you may feel like you're working well, but you're actually spending hours on one tiny detail.

If you're feeling stale, sometimes a change of scenery can help. You could try working in another room, or even outside if the weather is nice.

As an exercise, try doing a painting in 60 minutes. Don't worry if you don't finish it. Just get as far as you can. The more you try to work to a deadline, the better you'll get at meeting them!

Challenge Yourself

It's natural to want to stay in your comfort zone. If you enjoy painting flowers, then you could easily spend all your time painting flowers and become very good at it.

But if you want to develop as an artist and reach a point where you can draw or paint anything you want, you will need to challenge yourself. That means attempting projects that you know you will struggle with and may even fail at.

If you don't like the thought of this, remember that you've already challenged yourself before and succeeded many times. If you hadn't, you'd still be using crayons and drawing stick people.

So why not try something new? It could be a different kind of subject, or even a new medium. Don't listen to the voice inside your head saying you're not ready for that yet. If you don't try it, you never will be ready!

Once you start, you might find that it's not as difficult as it seems, and you can achieve more than you thought was possible. This will increase your self-confidence and build up your experience and skill.

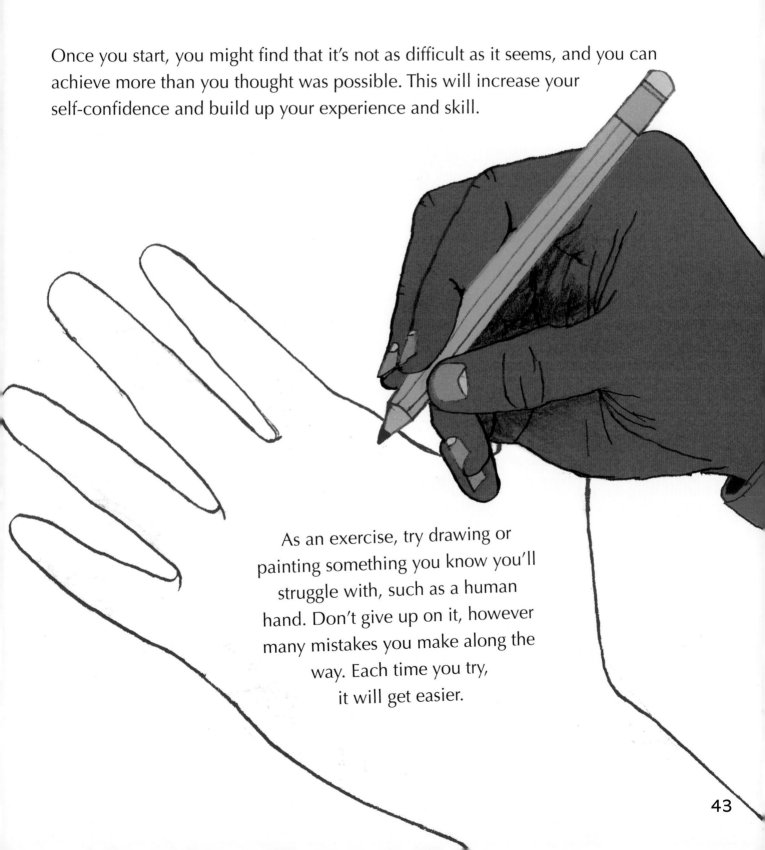

As an exercise, try drawing or painting something you know you'll struggle with, such as a human hand. Don't give up on it, however many mistakes you make along the way. Each time you try, it will get easier.

Don't Expect Perfection

You have a vision in your head about what your artwork should look like. It looks perfect. You want that vision to be what you end up creating, but it never is, and you feel disappointed.

It's always good to aim high, but don't feel bad if you don't achieve your goal. No art is perfect, because we aren't perfect. Neither are the tools and materials we use.

If you find you're anxious to create something perfect, it may be because you fear you are not measuring up to people's expectations. Or it may be because you are comparing yourself to other artists.

The trouble with expecting perfection is that it can hold you back. You might never start on a piece, because you don't have quite the right materials or you feel that you haven't done enough preparation.

If you are hoping for perfection, you may never stop working on a piece because it's never as good as you imagined it would be. But if you work on anything for too long, you could end up ruining it.

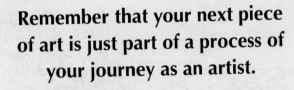

I still haven't finished...

If you feel yourself falling into these patterns of thinking, try taking the pressure off yourself. Remind yourself that you are here to have fun, to experiment, and to learn. No one is expecting a masterpiece.

Remember that your next piece of art is just part of a process of your journey as an artist.

Now that you have read this book, you've got all the information you need to start thinking like an artist. So don't wait any longer. The world of art is waiting for you!

Glossary

abstract art Art that does not attempt to show reality, but tries to achieve its effect by using shapes, colors, and textures

collage A piece of art made by sticking pieces of different materials together

composition The arrangement of the different parts of a picture

contrasting Differences in color, tone, or shape that add to the effect of an artwork

emancipated Freed from slavery

highlight A bright area in a painting or drawing

ink-wash A style of Asian painting that uses black ink applied with a brush

medium The material used by an artist, such as paint (for a painter) or stone (for a sculptor)

mixed-media Artwork that uses more than one medium

mosaic A picture or pattern produced by arranging together small pieces of stone, glass, or other materials

mural A large picture painted on a wall

origami The Japanese art of folding paper into shapes and figures

perspective The art of representing 3-D objects on a flat surface

prejudices Preconcieved opinions of someone or something, especially based on race

proportion The relationship of one part of a picture to another part in terms of size

radical Something that is extreme or drastic

review To examine or go over something again

sculpture An artwork that has three dimensions: height, width, and depth

subject The person or thing that is the focus of a work of art

texture The feel or appearance of a surface or substance

tonal Relating to the tone, or the brightness, deepness, or shade of a color

tuberculosis An infectious disease that often affects the lungs

Western Ideas or art originating in Europe or the New World

Learning More

Books

Amazing Artists. J.P. Miller. Crabtree Publishing, 2021.
This inspiring introduction to amazing Black artists gives readers an idea of what inspires artists and how they learn their craft.

Art Skills Lab (series). Various authors. Crabtree Publishing, 2020.
Use these how-to books to expand your art skills and use techniques across different mediums such as drawing, painting, collage, mixed media, and printmaking.

Inside Art Movements (series). Susie Brooks. Wayland, 2018.
Discover the art movements that shaped our world in this wonderfully visual series.
Titles include *Pop Art, Romanticism, Cubism, Surrealism, The Renaissance,* and *Impressionism.*

Websites

www.metmuseum.org/art/online-features/metkids
The #MetKids website allows you to explore New York City's famous Metropolitan Museum of Art using an interactive map. It includes videos, a "time machine" taking you through 5,000 years of art, fun facts, creative projects, and the #MetKids blog.

www.bbc.co.uk/bitesize/subjects/zn3rkqt
This website from the BBC contains tons of information, video clips, and games about art. It covers drawing, painting, sculpture and textiles; visual elements such as color, line, and shape, as well as artistic media, materials, and art history.

www.artforkidshub.com/how-to-draw
Simple and fun videos show you how to draw different objects, including a puppy, a witch, a cupcake, a zombie pizza, a black cat, a fish skeleton, and many more.

www.tate.org.uk/kids
This website from the Tate Britain museum features online galleries, games, quizzes, activities, and lessons on art, as well as videos about great artists and art movements.

Index